THE CHRISTMAS PUDDING JOKE BOOK

First woman:
'What's your husband getting for Christmas?'
Second woman:
'Fat and bald.'

The Christmas Pudding Joke Book

by Holly Berry

Illustrated by Mark Burgess

MAMMOTH

First published in Great Britain in 1989
by Mammoth, an imprint of Reed Consumer Books Limited
Michelin House, 81 Fulham Road, London SW3 6RB
and Auckland, Melbourne, Singapore and Toronto

Reprinted 1989, 1990, 1993

Text copyright © 1989 Martyn Forrester
Illustrations copyright © 1989 by Mark Burgess

ISBN 0 7497 0040 8

A CIP catalogue record for this title is available
from the British Library

Photoset in Linotron Century Schoolbook by
Rowland Phototypesetting Ltd,
Bury St Edmunds, Suffolk

Printed in Great Britain by
Cox & Wyman Ltd, Reading, Berkshire

Other joke books include:

Knock, knock!
– *Who's there?*
Mary.
– *Mary who?*
Mary Christmas everybody!

What does Tarzan sing at Christmas?
'Jungle bells, jungle bells . . .'

Knock, knock!
– *Who's there?*
Wayne.
– *Wayne who?*
Wayne in a manger . . .

Knock, knock!
– *Who's there?*
Oakham.
– *Oakham who?*
Oakham all ye faithful . . .

Knock, knock!
– *Who's there?*
Wendy.
– *Wendy who?*
Wendy red, red robin comes bob, bob,
bobbin' along . . .

(LOONY CAROL – SUNG TO THE
TUNE OF WE THREE KINGS)
Three wise men in Leicester Square,
Selling knickers, tuppence a pair;
They're fantastic,
No elastic,
Buy your Granny a pair . . .

Knock, knock!
– *Who's there?*
Dexter.
– *Dexter who?*
Dexter halls with boughs of holly . . .

What do witches sing at Christmas?
'Deck the halls with poison ivy . . .'

What does Dracula sing at Christmas?
'I'm dreaming of a fright Christmas . . .'

What is there in December that there
isn't in any other month?
The letter D.

What do elephants sing at Christmas?
'No-elephants, No-elephants . . .'

What do football fans sing at Christmas?
'Yule never walk alone . . .'

What did Noah sing at Christmas?
''Ark the herald angels sing . . .'

Knock, knock!
– *Who's there?*
Wenceslas.
– *Wenceslas who?*
Wenceslas bus home on Christmas Eve?

What do slimmers sing at Christmas?
'A weigh in a manger . . .'

I'll tell you what I like about Christmas
– kissing the girls under the mistletoe.
*Really? I prefer kissing them under
the nose.*

Why are Christmas trees
always warm?
Because they're fir trees.

1st cannibal woman:
My husband's always moaning about
Christmas. I don't know what to
make of him.
2nd cannibal woman:
How about a casserole?

Which burn longer, the candles on a
birthday cake or the candles on a
Christmas cake?
Neither – all candles burn shorter.

What Christmas carol is popular in the desert?
'O camel ye faithful . . .'

Knock, knock!
– *Who's there?*
Watson.
– *Watson who?*
Watson television on Christmas Eve?

What did one Christmas cracker say to the other Christmas cracker?
'I bet my pop's bigger than your pop!'

What do you call a tug-of-war on
24 December?
Christmas Heave.

Who gets the sack on Christmas Eve?
Santa Claus, of course!

What is Christmas called in
Great Britain?
Yule Britannia.

What nationality is Santa?
North Polish!

Why is it difficult to keep a secret at the
North Pole?
Because your teeth chatter.

How does Santa dress
at the North Pole?
Quickly!

What do you call a letter that is posted
up the chimney at Christmas?
Blackmail.

What do you keep even if you
give it away?
A cold.

What is a fjord?
A Norwegian motorcar.

What is the difference between the
North Pole and the South Pole?
All the difference in the world.

What kind of fish is most useful at the North Pole?
A skate.

How do you make a Mexican chilli?
Take him to the North Pole.

What is brown, has a large hump, and is found at the North Pole?
A lost camel.

What do angry mice send
each other at Christmas?
Cross-mouse cards!

What do angels write on their Christmas
cards?
'Halo everybody!'

What do monsters write on their
Christmas cards?
'Best vicious of the season.'

What do Christmas bells write on their
Christmas cards?
'Let's ring each other in the New Year.'

What do sheep write in their Christmas
cards?
'Merry Christmas to ewe.'

What does Santa write on his
Christmas cards?
*ABCDEFGHIJK
MNOPQRSTUVWXYZ — (No L, geddit?)*

What do cats write on their Christmas
cards?
*'Wishing you a furry merry Christmas
and a Happy Mew Year.'*

What did Adam write on his Christmas
card?
'Merry Christmas, Eve.'

What do Eskimos buy their
Christmas presents with?
Ice lolly.

What did the Eskimo wife sing when
her husband asked what they were
having for dinner?
'Whale meat again . . .'

Why do Eskimos eat candles?
Because they prefer light meals.

What cereal does an Eskimo have
for breakfast?
Snowflakes.

What does an Eskimo eat for a
Christmas snack?
Ice bergers.

Where do Eskimos get their milk from?
Eskimoos.

What do you call an Eskimo's house
without a loo?
An ig.

How does an Eskimo build a house?
Igloos it together.

Why did the little Eskimo girl bury her
father in the snow?
Because she liked cold pop.

What is a mushroom?
A place where Eskimos train huskies.

What message hangs above
an Eskimo's mantlepiece?
'Snow place like home . . .'

Why did the Eskimo girl get rid of her
boyfriend?
*He gave her an icy look so she gave him
the cold shoulder.*

Knock, knock!
– Who's there?
Igloo.
– Igloo who?
Igloo knew Suzie like I know Suzie . . .

What does a skeleton serve his Christmas
dinner on?
Bone china.

What's brown and steaming and comes at
you from all sides?
Stereophonic Christmas pudding.

What's brown and steaming and
travels along the seabed?
A Christmas pudding in a submarine.

Vicar: Did you say your prayers before
Christmas dinner, John?
John: No, sir, my Mum's a good cook.

What's brown and steaming and wears
sunglasses?
A Christmas pudding on holiday.

What's brown and steaming and goes up
and down?
A Christmas pudding in a lift.

What's brown and steaming
and goes slam-slam-slam-slam?
A four-door Christmas pudding.

Boy: I don't like this Christmas pudding.
Woman: Oh don't you? I'll have you know
I was making Christmas puddings
before you were born.
Boy: Perhaps this is one of them.

This Christmas pudding is nice
and warm.
It should be—the cat's been sitting on it!

What fruit do you find on coins?
Dates.

What is the best thing to put into
Christmas cake?
Your teeth.

What sugar sings?
I–sing sugar.

What's yellow and sweet and swings
from Christmas cake to Christmas cake?
Tarzipan.

'Mum, there's a black cat in the kitchen.'
'That's all right, black cats are lucky.'
'Not this one, he's just eaten the
Christmas dinner.'

When is Christmas pudding musical?
When it's piping hot.

How do monkeys know the date?
They eat it.

What's brown and steaming and highly
dangerous?
Shark-infested Christmas pudding.

What does Mrs Santa cook her
Christmas cake with?
Elf-raising flour!

What are brown and round and sneak
around the kitchen?
Mince spies!

Which town in Britain sells bad meat to
go with your turkey?
Oldham.

Why did the banana go out with the
prune?
Because he couldn't find a date.

Why is Christmas pudding like the sea?
Because it's full of currants.

What would you get if you crossed
an apple with a Christmas tree?
A pineapple.

What do cannibals eat for Christmas
dinner?
Baked beings with Swedes.

Knock, knock!
– *Who's there?*
Doughnut.
– *Doughnut who?*
Doughnut open until December 25th!

Knock, knock!
– *Who's there?*
Felix.
– *Felix who?*
Felix my mince pie once more I'll scream!

Knock, knock!
– *Who's there?*
Arthur.
– *Arthur who?*
Arthur any mince pies left?

What's brown and steaming and goes round and round?
A Christmas pudding in a spin-drier.

Why is history the sweetest lesson?
Because it's full of dates.

Which of Santa's helpers is small, has pointed ears, and solves crimes?
Sherlock Gnomes.

Where do gnomes do their shopping?
British Gnome Stores.

Why didn't Santa's helpers go
on holiday abroad?
Because they got gnomesick.

What do Santa's helpers say when
they get back to the North Pole
after delivering the presents on
Christmas Eve?
Gnome, sweet gnome.

What happened when the Christmas
Fairy ate a tree decoration by mistake?
She got tinselitis.

Why can only tiny fairies sit under
toadstools?
Because there isn't mushroom.

What do Santa's elves like
to eat for tea?
Fairy cakes.

Which sort of elf eats its food quickly?
A goblin.

Who helps sick fairies and gnomes?
The National Elf Service.

Where do the fairies go to recover after
working so hard in the Toy Factory?
Elf farms.

What do cold geese suffer from?
Goose pimples!

What is a goose's favourite food?
Gooseberries, of course!

Knock, knock!
– *Who's there?*
Goose.
– *Goose who?*
Goose who's knocking at your door?

Knock, knock!
– *Who's there?*
Gander.
– *Gander who?*
I be-gander wonder if you'd ever answer!

What is a Laplander?
A clumsy person on a bus.

How does Jack Frost get to work?
By icicle.

What happens when you slip on the ice?
Your bottom gets thaw.

What sort of sheet cannot be folded?
A sheet of ice.

Teacher: Name one animal
that lives in Lapland.
Pupil: A reindeer.
Teacher: Good. Now name another.
Pupil: Another reindeer.

How do sheep keep warm at the
North Pole?
By central bleating.

What do you get if you cross a hush puppy
with ice?
A slush puppy.

What do monsters like best about the
North Pole?
Slay-riding.

Why do birds fly south in winter?
Because it's too far to walk.

A tourist in Lapland saw an
advertisement for a restaurant which
claimed that any dish requested could be
served, no matter how strange. The man
decided to visit the restaurant to test out
the claim. When he was seated at a table
he asked for reindeer and chips. The
waiter took this order calmly, and went
away into the kitchen. A few minutes
later the waiter returned and said, 'I'm
awfully sorry, sir, but we seem to have
run out of potatoes . . .'

How do you make anti-freeze?
Send her to the North Pole.

What do you call an alligator
at the North Pole?
A cold snap.

What water won't freeze at the
North Pole?
Boiling water.

What is the hardest thing about learning
to skate?
The ice.

What's the difference between an
iceberg and a clothes brush?
*One crushes boats and the other
brushes coats.*

What is ice?
Skid stuff.

What is the coldest country
in the world?
Chile.

How can you spell chilly using just two
letters?
I C

What do you call someone whose father
was born at the North Pole and whose
mother was born in Cuba?
An ice cube.

What do you call a witch at the
North Pole?
A cold spell.

What sort of athlete would be
warmest at the North Pole?
A long jumper.

What wears a coat all winter and
pants all summer?
A dog.

Why shouldn't you read *The Christmas
Pudding Joke Book* while you're
ice-skating?
The ice might crack up.

What travels faster, heat or cold?
Heat — it's easy to catch cold.

Knock, knock!
– *Who's there?*
Martini.
– *Martini who?*
Martini hands are frozen . . .

What's big and icy and tastes delicious?
A glacier mint.

What goes out black and comes back
white?
A black cow in a snowstorm.

Which football team do squirrels play in?
Nuts Forest.

What sort of horse is an old joke?
A chestnut.

What nut sounds like a sneeze?
Cashew.

What nut has no shell?
A doughnut.

What is the best way to keep nuts?
Don't return them.

What nut might you hang a picture on?
A walnut.

What nut is found by the sea?
The beechnut.

What did the hazelnut say to
the reindeer?
Nothing – hazelnuts can't talk, silly!

How do you catch an elephant?
*Hide a big net behind your back and make
a noise like a peanut.*

What did Cinderella sing when her
photographs weren't ready?
'Some day my prints will come . . .'

Why was Cinderella banned from the
hockey team?
*Because she kept running away from
the ball.*

Why did Robin Hood only steal from
rich people?
*Because poor people didn't have anything
to steal.*

Knock, knock!
– Who's there?
Godfrey.
– Godfrey who?
Godfrey tickets for the pantomime!

Why was Cinderella such
a bad football player?
She had a pumpkin for a coach.

On which side of the house did Jack's
beanstalk grow?
On the outside.

What kind of pet did Aladdin have?
A flying car-pet!

Why did the farmer call his cockerel
Robinson?
Because he crew so.

What did one flea on Robinson
Crusoe say to the other flea?
'Bye for now, see you on Friday.'

Who on Treasure Island has a parrot
that cries 'Pieces of four'?
Short John Silver.

Who invented the five-day week?
*Robinson Crusoe – he had all his work
done by Friday!*

Who shouted 'Knickers!' at the
big bad wolf?
Little Rude Riding Hood.

Knock, knock!
– *Who's there?*
Aladdin.
– *Aladdin who?*
Aladdin the park is looking for you.

What is beautiful, grey and wears
glass slippers?
Cinderellephant.

What gives milk and makes all your
dreams come true?
Your Dairy Godmother.

Who wears a crown, lives in a
supermarket, and calls for his
fiddlers three?
Old King Cole Slaw.

Did you hear about the actor who was so
eager to get the part of Long John Silver
that he had his leg cut off?
*He still didn't get the job – it was the
wrong leg.*

Who looked after Finderella?
Her Fairy Codmother.

What is a ghost's favourite Christmas
entertainment?
The phantomime.

Who sailed the seven seas looking for
rubbish and blubber?
Binbag the Whaler.

Which is the scariest pantomime?
Ghouldilocks and the Three Brrrrrs.

Which member of Robin Hood's
band was Welsh?
Rhyl Scarlet.

Which pantomime is set in a
chemist's shop?
Puss in Boots.

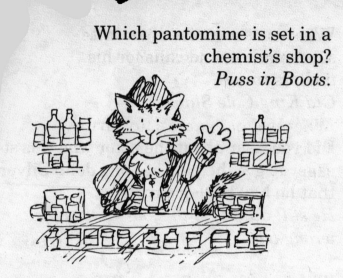

What did the guests sing at the Eskimo's
Christmas party?
'Freeze a jolly good fellow . . .'

What did the guests sing at the Scottish
Christmas party?
'Ivy long to Glasgow . . .'

Where do astronauts kiss each other at
the Christmas party?
Under the missile-toe.

What is a horse's favourite
Christmas party game?
Stable tennis.

What is a crocodile's favourite
Christmas party game?
Snap.

What is a kangaroo's favourite
Christmas party game?
Hop-scotch.

What is a monster's favourite
Christmas party game?
Corpse and robbers.

What is a cannibal's favourite
Christmas party game?
Swallow my leader.

What is Scrooge's favourite
Christmas party game?
Meanopoly.

What is a glum person's favourite
Christmas party game?
Moanopoly.

What is a frog's favourite
Christmas party game?
Croquet.

What is a mouse's favourite
Christmas party game?
Hide and squeak.

What game do cows like to play at
Christmas parties?
Moo-sical chairs.

What goes black and white,
black and white, black and white,
black and white?
A penguin rolling down a hill.

What do you get if you cross a penguin
with a sheep?
A sheepskin dinner jacket.

What bird can write underwater?
A ballpoint penguin.

What's black and white and makes a
dreadful noise?
A penguin playing the bag-pipes.

What's black and white and bounces?
A penguin on a pogo stick.

What's black and white and
goes round and round?
A penguin in a revolving door.

What's black and white and red all over?
A sunburnt penguin.

What's black and white and blue all over?
A zebra at the North Pole.

What's black and white and noisy?
*A penguin who got a drumkit for
Christmas.*

What is big, white and found in the
desert?
A lost polar bear.

How can you save money on pet food?
Get a polar bear – he lives on ice!

What did the polar bear have for lunch?
Ice bergers.

How do you get fur from a polar bear?
Run fast in the opposite direction.

What's white, furry, and smells of peppermint?
A polo bear.

'Mummy,' said the baby polar bear, 'am I 100% pure polar bear?'
'Of course you are, son,' said his mother. 'Why do you ask?'
'Because I'm flippin' freezing!'

What do you get if you cross a polar bear with a kangaroo?
A fur coat with enormous pockets.

Why don't polar bears eat penguins?
Because they can't get the wrappers off.

Why do polar bears have fur coats?
*Because they'd look silly
in plastic macs.*

What do you need to spot a polar bear
half a mile away?
Very good ice-sight.

What's big, white and furry, and found
in Liverpool?
A polar bear that's lost.

What did the polar bear take
on holiday?
Just the bear essentials.

Where does a two ton polar bear sleep?
Anywhere he wants to.

What do you call a smelly polar bear?
Winnie the Pooh.

Did you hear the sad story about
the two polar bears?
Their marriage is on the rocks.

What do you call a polar bear in
ear-muffs?
Anything you like, he can't hear you.

Did you hear about the woman who
wanted something with diamonds
for Christmas?
*Her husband bought her a pack of
playing cards.*

Did you hear about the woman who
wanted an animal skin coat for Christmas?
Her husband bought her a donkey jacket.

The bottle of perfume that Willie sent
Was highly displeasing to Millicent.
Her thanks were so cold
That they quarrelled, I'm told.
Through that silly scent Willie
sent Millicent.

What happened when the man
swallowed the watch he'd been
given for Christmas?
He found it very time-consuming.

'Doctor, doctor, my wife's just swallowed
the pen I gave her for Christmas.
What shall I do?'
'Use a pencil.'

I didn't find any Christmas presents this
year. My stocking had a big hole.

'What is your husband getting for
Christmas?'
'Fat and bald.'

My brother is a boy of rare gifts. He hasn't
given one for years.

Did you hear about the woman who
wanted a 12-piece silver set for Christmas?
*Her husband gave her eleven 10Ps
and a 5P.*

Did you hear about the woman who wanted something for her neck for Christmas?
Her husband bought her a cake of soap.

What do you give the man who has everything?
A burglar alarm.

'What did you get for Christmas?'
'A barometer made in Japan.'
'Who wants to know what the weather's like in Tokyo?'

'What are you giving your little sister for Christmas?'
'I don't know yet. Last year I gave her the measles.'

'Why did you send me an empty box for my Christmas present?'
'At least when I send you nothing I wrap it up nicely.'

Knock, knock!
– *Who's there?*
Fiona.
– *Fiona who?*
Fiona had some money I could buy
you a Christmas present.

Knock, knock!
– *Who's there?*
Noise.
– *Noise who?*
Noise to see a full stocking on Christmas
morning.

How many presents can Santa fit
into an empty sack measuring
a metre by a metre?
*Only one – after that it's not empty
any more.*

Mother: Would you like a pocket
calculator for Christmas?
Son: No thank you.
Mother: Why not?
Son: Because I already know how many
pockets I have.

What did Santa give the octopus
for Christmas?
Four pairs of gloves.

What did Santa give the deaf fisherman
for Christmas?
A herring aid.

What is the difference between teachers
and Christmas presents?
Children love Christmas presents.

Where does a plumber do his
Christmas shopping?
Bath.

Where is the best place to buy
your dog a Christmas present?
Leeds.

Where does Noddy do his
Christmas shopping?
Redcar.

Where does a gardener do his
Christmas shopping?
Barrow.

Where does the Queen do her
Christmas shopping?
Newcastle.

Who delivered the cat's Christmas
presents?
Santa Paws.

Who delivered the cat's other
Christmas present?
Santa Claws.

Why did the boy's mother knit him three
socks for Christmas?
Because he'd grown another foot.

What's the best Christmas present?
Well, a drumkit takes a lot of beating . . .

1st Boy: The best Christmas present I
ever got was a drumkit.
2nd Boy: Why's that?
1st Boy: My father still gives me 20p a
week not to play it.

What did the witch
want for Christmas?
A witch watch.

What did the miser give his wife
for Christmas?
A ladder in her stocking.

What did the ungrateful boy say
when he got a violin for Christmas?
'Oh fiddle . . .'

What does a reindeer say before he
tells a joke?
'This one will sleigh you!'

Two reindeer were talking. One asked the
other, 'How was the stag party?'

The mother turkey was scolding her
children for being naughty. 'You bad
children,' she said, 'if your father could
hear you he'd turn in his gravy.'

What did Santa say to his wife on
Christmas Eve?
'Don't go out in the reindeer.'

What do you give a reindeer with
indigestion?
Elka-seltzer.

What do you call a reindeer
with one eye?
No idea.

What do you call a reindeer that doesn't
move, and has one eye?
Still no idea.

'I don't care who you are – get those
reindeer off my roof!'

'What is the use of reindeer?'
'*It makes the garden grow, sweetie.*'

'How many legs does Rudolph have?'
'*Four.*'
'No, six – he's got forelegs and
two back legs.'

What game do six reindeer play in the
back of a Mini?
Squash.

Why did Rudolph take his red nose apart?
To see what made it run.

What do you call a reindeer with a number on its tail?
Reg.

Did you hear the story of the three reindeer?
No? Oh dear, dear, dear.

HO, HO, HO.

Why do reindeer have wrinkled ankles?
Because they lace their boots too tight.

How many chimneys does Santa have to climb down each Christmas?
Stacks.

Why did Father Christmas have
to go to a psychiatrist?
He didn't believe in himself.

Why does Santa have a garden?
Because he likes to hoe-hoe-hoe.

What is Santa's favourite TV
programme?
Hawaii Five-Ho Ho Ho.

What's the last thing Santa takes
off when he finally goes to bed
on Christmas Eve?
His feet off the floor.

What did Santa do when he locked
himself out of the toy factory?
*He whistled a tune until he found
the right key.*

Why does Santa always climb down
chimneys?
Because it soots him.

What kind of exams did Santa Claus pass?
His ho-ho-ho levels.

Who do elephants get their Christmas
presents from?
Elephanta Claus.

1st Boy: What is Santa's wife called?
2nd Boy: Mrs Santa?
1st Boy: No, Mary Christmas!

Why is a cat in the desert like Father Christmas?
Because of its Sandy Claws.

What do you get if you cross Father Christmas with Sherlock Holmes?
Santa Clues.

Why does Santa wear a red coat?
Because his blue one is at the cleaners.

Why does Santa wear red braces?
To keep his trousers up.

What would happen if Minnehaha
married Father Christmas?
She'd change her name to Minnehoho.

What goes, 'Ho, ho, ho, bonk?'
Father Christmas laughing his head off.

Why does Father Christmas's wife stay at
home on Christmas Eve?
She has to do her Santa Chores.

Why is Santa like a bear on
Christmas Eve?
Because he's Sooty.

Where do snowmen go dancing?
At the snowball.

What's black and white
and red all over?
Santa falling down the chimney.

What does Father Christmas suffer from
if he gets stuck in the chimney?
Santa Claustrophobia.

Knock, knock!
– *Who's there?*
Snow.
– *Snow who?*
Snow use asking me, *I* don't know.

What do you get if you cross
a shark with a snowman?
Frostbite!

What did the snowman say to himself
while he was dancing?
'Snow, snow, quick quick, snow . . .'

What is a cold war?
A snowball fight.

What is ploughed but never planted?
Snow.

When is a boat like a heap of snow?
When it is adrift.

Did you hear the joke about the
snowman?
It would leave you cold.

Why was the turkey sitting on an axe?
She was trying to hatchet.

What do you call a bird that steals?
Robin.

Knock, knock!
– *Who's there?*
Snow.
– *Snow who?*
Snow business like show business . . .

Why does Mrs Santa wear curlers in bed
on Christmas Eve?
*Because she wants to wake up curly in the
morning.*

What bird is always around when you eat
your Christmas dinner?
A swallow.

Did you hear about the wally turkey?
He was looking forward to Christmas.

On which side does a turkey have most feathers?
On the outside.

What do turkeys like on television?
Duckumentaries.

How do turkeys communicate?
They use fowl language.

What goes, 'Gobble, gobble, bang'?
A turkey in a minefield.

Why did the family of eight
cross a turkey with an octopus?
*So everyone got a leg for
Christmas dinner.*

Why did the turkey cross the road?
To prove he wasn't chicken.

Where is the best place to go for
Christmas dinner?
Turkey.

Noah: I thought we had two turkeys
when we set sail?
Mrs Noah: Well dear, it is Christmas . . .

Why is a turkey like an evil little
creature?
Because it's always a-gobblin'.

Why did the turkey cross the road?
Because it was the chicken's day off.

'We had our Granny for Christmas
this year.'
'Really? We had turkey.'

Why did the blind turkey cross the road?
To get to the Bird's Eye shop.

What made the boy turkey fall in love
with the girl turkey?
She egged him on.

'I've lost my turkey. What should I do?'
'Call the Flying Squad.'

What is a turkey's favourite TV
programme?
The feather forecast.

Why are turkeys wiser than chickens?
Ever heard of Kentucky Fried Turkey?

How do turkeys dance?
Chick to chick.

What do you get if you cross a
chicken with a turkey?
A churkey.

Did you hear about the turkey farmer
who installed a gobblestone driveway?

'Mummy, Mummy, can I have a puppy for
Christmas?'
'No, you can have turkey like everyone else.'

Who is never hungry at Christmas?
The turkey – he's always stuffed.

What bird has wings but cannot fly?
Roast turkey.

Why was the turkey allowed to join the
pop group?
Because he had two drumsticks.

What do ghouls put on their turkey at
Christmas?
Grave-y.

What do you call a baby turkey?
A goblet.

What should all your friends give
you for telling them so many
excellent Christmas jokes?
A big round of Santapplause!

CHRISTMAS BOOKS

Off To Market . . . . Tobias A. Turkey
Christmas Kisses . . . . Miss L. Toe
Ding Dong Merrily On High . . . .
  Belle Ringer
Small Stables For Big
  Reindeer . . . . Maureen Thanout
Fun in the Snow . . . . S. K. Moe
Aladdin . . . . Jeannie F. T. Lamp
Off to the Panto . . . . I. Felix Cited

The Christmas Party's Over . . . .
  Olga Home
Christmas Hangover . . . .
  Ivan Aiken Head
Puss In Boots . . . . Kitty Wellshod

Should you ever kiss under the mistletoe
with your eyes closed?
No – it's better with your lips.

Knock, knock!
– Who's there?
Sherwood.
– Sherwood who?
Sherwood like to kiss you under the
mistletoe.

What did the tomato say to
the cucumber under the mistletoe?
'Lettuce alone.'

What did the boy teddy bear say to the
girl teddy bear under the mistletoe?
'Let's go teddy!'

What did the boy octopus say to the girl
octopus under the mistletoe?
'I want to hold your hand, hand, hand,
hand, hand, hand . . .'

What did the invisible man say to his
invisible girlfriend under the mistletoe?
'It's lovely not to see you again.'

What did the Egyptian mummy say
to his girlfriend under the mistletoe?
'Em-balmy about you.'

If a waiter carrying a turkey on a platter
lets it fall, what three great national
disasters occur?
*The downfall of Turkey, the break-up of
China, and the overthrow of Greece.*

Why is the turkey such a fashionable
bird?
*Because he always appears well-dressed
for dinner.*

Did you hear about the man who was so
rich he bought his puppy a boy for
Christmas?

What did the duck say when it had
finished its Christmas shopping?
'Just put it on my bill.'

The shortest night of the year for
parents is Christmas Eve – from
sundown to son up.

What is Rudolph the Red-nosed
Reindeer's favourite aeroplane?
Conk-cord.

Who is Father Christmas's favourite
pop star?
Sister Sledge.

Why might Santa not be able to bring
presents next year?
Because he got the sack.

What did the artist Vincent
van Gogh want for Christmas?
A Happy New Ear.

Wife: Why did you buy me such a tiny
diamond for Christmas?
Husband: I didn't want the glare to hurt
your eyes.

What did one lumberjack say to the other
lumberjack?
*'Only five more chopping days to
Christmas.'*

Boy: Just think – tomorrow is Christmas
and a year ago I didn't even know you.
Girl: Never mind about our past – what
about my present?

What happened when the two ghosts
kissed under the mistletoe?
It was love at first fright.

What did the skeleton say to his girlfriend
under the mistletoe?
'I love every bone in your body.'

What did the beaver say to
the Christmas tree?
'It's been nice gnawing you.'

Knock, knock!
– *Who's there?*
Ken.
– *Ken who?*
Ken I kiss you under the mistletoe?

What did the girl vegetable say to the boy
vegetable under the mistletoe?
'Will you be my swedeheart?'

What has a mouth but never kisses
under the mistletoe?
A river.

What did the bull say to his girlfriend
under the mistletoe?
'When I fall in love, it will be for heifer . . .'

What did the ram say to his girlfriend under the mistletoe?
'*I love ewe.*'

What did Lady Hamilton say to Lord Nelson under the mistletoe?
'*You're the one-eye care for!*'

Girl: Mum, is it dangerous to kiss under the mistletoe?
Mother: It certainly is. I got your father that way.

Angry Girl to boy under mistletoe: Who said you could kiss me?
Boy: Everybody.

Girl: Am I the first girl you've ever kissed under the mistletoe?
Boy: Maybe – your face looks familiar.

How do hedgehogs kiss under the mistletoe?
Very carefully.

What is found at the end of every year?
The letter R.

What was the caterpillar's New Year's resolution?
To turn over a new leaf.

While every effort is made to keep prices low, it is sometimes necessary to increase prices at short notice. Mandarin Paperbacks reserves the right to show new retail prices on covers which may differ from those previously advertised in the text or elsewhere.

The prices shown below were correct at the time of going to press.

☐	7497 0366 0	**Dilly the Dinosaur**	Tony Bradman	£2.50
☐	7497 0137 4	**Flat Stanley**	Jeff Brown	£2.50
☐	7497 0306 7	**The Chocolate Touch**	P Skene Catling	£2.50
☐	7497 0568 X	**Dorrie and the Goblin**	Patricia Coombs	£2.50
☐	7497 0114 5	**Dear Grumble**	W J Corbett	£2.50
☐	7497 0054 8	**My Naughty Little Sister**	Dorothy Edwards	£2.50
☐	7497 0723 2	**The Little Prince (colour ed.)**	A Saint-Exupery	£3.99
☐	7497 0305 9	**Bill's New Frock**	Anne Fine	£2.99
☐	7497 0590 6	**Wild Robert**	Diana Wynne Jones	£2.50
☐	7497 0661 9	**The Six Bullerby Children**	Astrid Lindgren	£2.50
☐	7497 0319 9	**Dr Monsoon Taggert's Amazing Finishing Academy**	Andrew Matthews	£2.50
☐	7497 0420 9	**I Don't Want To!**	Bel Mooney	£2.50
☐	7497 0833 6	**Melanie and the Night Animal**	Gillian Rubinstein	£2.50
☐	7497 0264 8	**Akimbo and the Elephants**	A McCall Smith	£2.50
☐	7497 0048 3	**Friends and Brothers**	Dick King-Smith	£2.50
☐	7497 0795 X	**Owl Who Was Afraid of the Dark**	Jill Tomlinson	£2.99

All these books are available at your bookshop or newsagent, or can be ordered direct from the publisher. Just tick the titles you want and fill in the form below.

Mandarin Paperbacks, Cash Sales Department, PO Box 11, Falmouth, Cornwall TR10 9EN.

Please send cheque or postal order, no currency, for purchase price quoted and allow the following for postage and packing:

UK including BFPO   £1.00 for the first book, 50p for the second and 30p for each additional book ordered to a maximum charge of £3.00.

Overseas including Eire   £2 for the first book, £1.00 for the second and 50p for each additional book thereafter.

NAME (Block letters) ....

ADDRESS ....

....

☐ I enclose my remittance for ....

☐ I wish to pay by Access/Visa Card Number

Expiry Date